"Dedicated to God, whose love lights our way.

To my amazing parents, your love and support mean everything. Thank you for always being there.

With love and gratitude, this book is for you."

Eliésio Oliveira

2024

# This Book Belongs to:

# Test Color Page